An Executive Personal Development Series

The Extreme Minimalist

Discovering the Joys of Minimalism and Frugality

Thejendra Sreenivas

Book Publishing Coach
www.thejendra.com

Copyright © 2026 Thejendra Sreenivas

Second Edition: 2026

All rights reserved. No part of this publication may be reproduced, distributed, or transmitted in any form or by any means, including photocopying, recording, or other electronic or mechanical methods, without the prior written permission of the author or publisher, except in the case of brief quotations embodied in critical reviews and certain other noncommercial uses permitted by copyright law.

Licensing – If you have purchased an eBook or a digital version of this book then it's licensed for your personal enjoyment only. It may not be re-sold or gifted to other people. If you would like to share this with others, please purchase an additional eBook for each person you share it with. If you are reading this and did not purchase it, or it was not purchased for your use only, then please purchase your own copy. Thank you for respecting the publisher's work.

Table of Contents

About the Series iii

Preface v

The Gift Incident 1

The Fear Factor 9

The Scary Questions 15

Lecture-1: The Big House Syndrome 21

Lecture-2: Downsizing and Retirement 31

Lecture-3: Cut the Clutter 35

Lecture-4: Stop Dreaming of that Glorious Day 39

Lecture-5: Stop Being a Spendthrift 45

Lecture-6: The Celebrity Myth 53

Lecture-7: The Smartphone Story 57

Lecture-8: Practical Examples 63

Some Magnificent Gems 67

Other Books by the Author 75

   Author Services 79

About the Author 81

About the Series

The **Executive Personal Development Series** is a set of short non-fiction books on business management, leadership, inspiration, motivation, and self-improvement topics. Each book is an imaginary discussion between a retired professor who thinks unconventionally and a corporate executive who thinks like the crowd. This is a unique professor who thinks, "What is popular may not be right, and what is right may not be popular."

Most self-help books are normally written in a textbook or step-by-step guide format. But these books are written like novels in a conversational style with interactive lectures, candid arguments, and idle talk between the two who belong to different generations. Each book discusses some self-improvement concept or an aspect of the executive's personal or professional life, and the professor enlightens, alters, or completely demolishes the executive's earlier thinking and assumptions.

The first book in the series is The Power of

Laziness, followed by The Extreme Minimalist and others. However, each book can be read independently.

Preface

"Hey, look at my new super smartphone."

"Looks great. How much did you pay for it?"

"Only $1000 after discount. The original price is $1200. Why don't you also buy one?"

"Sorry, not interested."

"Why not? You can afford one, can't you?"

"Of course, but I am now saving money for a rainy day and my retirement."

"Your retirement? That's still 15-20 years away. Why bother now?"

"No, time travels fast, and bad days will come. This is why I am now a minimalist."

"Minimalist? Do you mean stinginess? What next? Will you have cold showers in the winter?"

"No, minimalism will ensure that I don't have cold showers in the winter."

The Gift Incident

After completing the amazing course on laziness, my life became magical. I was calmer and more productive than before, thanks to the great advice given by the wonderful professor and my stubborn friend who forced me to enroll in his workshop. But there was a strange emptiness now. It's rare to meet a person who has such a profound effect on you. It was fun when I was visiting him and listening to his pearls of wisdom. But I had learned everything about laziness and slowness, and there was no need to visit him again. Yet, I missed him and wanted to go back to him to learn something new. I called my friend who had introduced me to the professor and described the workshop experience.

"It was a wonderful experience, my well-wisher buddy. He was amazing. I must thank you for arm-twisting me into enrolling in his workshop."

"See, I told you he is great. I am glad you found it useful. I suggest you tell your other workaholic friends about his workshop."

"I will definitely spread the word."

"By the way, did you pay the professor for the course?"

"No, I asked him for the fee, but he evaded my question. But I should pay him something for this wonderful workshop."

"Why don't you give him a book? He loves books."

"Nah, he already has enough books. I will give him something better."

"What do you have in mind?"

"I noticed the professor still uses an ordinary phone. Maybe I will give him a good smartphone as a gift."

"Hmm, that's a good idea, but I don't think he will accept it. He lives a frugal life and doesn't accept expensive gifts."

"I will give it a try."

"Good luck, but don't bet on him accepting it."

Soon, I bought a nice big smartphone and visited the professor to thank him again for this amazing workshop and handed him the package.

"What's this?"

"A small gift for your wonderful workshop, professor."

"I am glad you liked my workshop. But I can't

accept this gift."

"No, professor. I insist you accept it."

After some pestering, he agreed to accept it.

"Fine, I will take it. What is it?"

"It's a smartphone."

"Thanks. How much did it cost?"

"Don't worry about that, professor."

"I insist you tell me."

"Only $1000."

"Only $1000? Isn't that expensive for a phone?"

"Actually, the original price is $1200. I got a discount because of my influence."

"Young chap, you shouldn't be throwing money like this. You should plan for your retirement."

"My retirement? That's still 15–20 years away, professor. Why bother now? Besides, I can afford it."

"No, time travels fast, and bad days will come. Frugality is necessary for everyone, even if you are earning well."

"You remind me of my penny-pinching father, professor. He would say the same statement again and again."

"Penny-pinching father? I would say he was a wise man."

"Wise? He was so tightfisted that getting some

pocket money from him was a nightmare. Even when I got my first bicycle or a bat, it was a used one while all my friends got a new one. It was so embarrassing."

"Stop demeaning your father. Maybe things were difficult, and that's why he was careful with money."

"Actually, he earned plenty of money but never loosened his purse strings. Even my mother supported him. But I don't want to do that to my kids. I want them to have the best my money can afford. Besides, things are quite easy to acquire now, unlike in the past."

"What do you mean easy?"

"I mean stuff like cars, phones, gadgets, etc., are all available in easy monthly installments. I don't have to pay the entire amount upfront. I even bought my new car like that last week."

"New car? What happened to your old one? Was it not working well?"

"No, it was in good condition."

"Then why did you sell it?"

"It was more than three years old. So, I exchanged that for this new one."

"Hmm, I presume this is also on nice easy installments?"

"Yes, I can complete the car payment within four

years. Even though it's a luxury premium model, my neighbor got me a great discount on it."

"Neighbor?"

"Yes, my neighbor in my new apartment works in this car company and he got me a discount. Even he drives the same brand and model."

"New apartment? So, you moved house also?"

"Not yet, but I am planning to move to a new bigger house."

"Why?"

"My current house is small and cannot accommodate my new furniture, car parking, etc. So, I have booked a new apartment. It will be a surprise for my family as they are always craving a big house."

"Hmm, all these new things must be quite a drain on your purse. What if you lose your job?"

"No problem. I am well qualified and can easily get another job, as I have plenty of contacts. Stop worrying, professor. You are thinking like a pessimist, just like my father used to."

"Maybe you should follow in some of his footsteps."

"But I don't want to become miserly like him, professor. We must lead a good life when we are earning well and not become stingy. I want to give my family the best possible life and not that ordinary life my miserly father gave me."

"I don't agree with you calling him miserly. I still say your father was a wise man. Life is not about continuously spending money, but also about saving for a rainy day."

"How was he wise, professor? He was penny-pinching even though he was earning tons of money. We could have lived a lavish life like our friends and relatives, but he never allowed us to."

"He was wise because he was a long-distance runner in life and not a short-distance runner like you. His eyes and mind could see life threats, risks, and dangers that you (and your friends and relatives) were unable or unwilling to see."

"Well, professor, I was never able to understand what was going on in my father's mind."

"I have a unique workshop to understand that (wink)."

"Another workshop? Is it a mind-reading workshop?"

"No, it's some advice and lectures designed to frighten today's executives."

"Frighten executives? Why do you want to scare them?"

"I feel it's necessary to frighten today's executives."

"Why? What will the frightening achieve?"

"I can't reveal it now. That's only for those who attend my fright workshop. Are you interested?"

"Hmm, your workshop sounds like a suspense movie, professor."

"I can give those lectures in the evenings. Join if you are free."

"I will try to come, professor."

The Fear Factor

I called my friend and told him about the trouble I had in making the professor accept my gift, the discussion about my father, and also about the new fright workshop. My friend laughed and said,

"Ah, here is a chance for you to visit the professor again. You were missing his wisdom, right?"

"Yes, but a course on fright is not exactly interesting. I am not sure if it will be as useful as the laziness course. But I am impressed by this professor and want to listen to his wise sayings again."

"Give it a try. Didn't he say that this workshop will help you understand what was going on in your father's mind to behave like a penny-pincher?"

"Hmm, that's a good suggestion. My father never explained why he was such a tightwad. Maybe this professor will reveal what was going on in my father's mind."

So, curious to know what this professor was going to preach, I visited him the next week.

"Hello, professor. I am back."

"Good. So, you have decided to attend my fright workshop."

"Yes, professor. I was curious to know why you frighten modern executives in this workshop."

"Yes, some fear is necessary. Are you ready?"

"Yes."

"Let me begin my first lecture with a recent news item. Mr. K was a real estate businessman and owned several properties in the city, including a resort on the outskirts. He also owned a big mansion in the most expensive area in the city. But he was recently arrested for killing his wife and then trying to kill his three children and then commit suicide."

"Shocking. Why did he do that?"

"According to the police, he had incurred a huge loss and was in debt. He had taken massive loans from multiple banks and several moneylenders who were after him for repayment. He wanted to clear the loans by selling his posh house and other properties but could not do so."

"Why?"

"His wife prevented him from selling the properties, and this led to bitter fights frequently. Soon, the arguments escalated, and the situation went out of hand as he was under enormous pressure and threats to repay the loans. But due to his wife's objection and refusal to sell the property, he went berserk and shot her dead and later attempted to kill his children and then commit suicide, but could not do so."

"Terrible. Why did his wife refuse to help him?"

"She did not want to reduce her standard of living and move to a small house."

"Wow! That is a sad story, professor. I remember reading this news item, and it was highly disturbing to me and my wife. He was a well-known businessman."

"Yes, it shocked countless people. Besides getting disturbed, what did you and your wife do after reading this terrible news?"

"Us? We didn't do anything. What were we supposed to do?"

"You could have discussed how you will handle your affairs if you get hit by the businessman's plight."

"Should we have discussed that?"

"Why not? What if you encounter the same situation as that businessman?"

"Well, professor, his case was different. I am not in that situation. That businessman and his wife should have taken precautions before the situation went out of hand."

"What precautions?"

"Maybe they could have saved some money."

"Yes, they should have. But why didn't they do it?"

"Why? I don't know why. We need to ask them."

"Okay, what if you meet a similar fate as that businessman and lose your job tomorrow? Will you be able to afford the monthly expenses and repay the big loans that you currently have?"

"I am well qualified and am confident that I can easily get another job, as I have plenty of contacts."

"Perhaps, but let's think of an extreme scenario. Suppose you don't get another job for several months or get a job in another city that you can't go to. Then, what will you do?"

"Hmm, then it will be difficult to afford the expenditure."

Then the professor dropped a few nuclear bombs.

"What if you die tomorrow or meet some terrible accident and become bedridden? What if you get some terminal illness and die one year from now? Can your family still continue your current lifestyle and all the luxuries you are currently enjoying? Can your family instantly downgrade their life?"

My heart skipped a beat. The harsh, straightforward questions shocked me, and I did not have an answer.

"No, professor. They will not be able to manage even for a few months," I answered sheepishly.

"I know, my dear chap. Most executives like you think that financial problems, bankruptcies, suicides, etc., only happen to some other people but not to you. So, you happily lead a lavish lifestyle and increase your standard of living. Secondly, you assume that your credentials, knowledge, and friends will keep you employed forever or help get new jobs. Or you think that your good deeds and positive thoughts will safeguard you.

Sadly, you are mistaken. Nature is nasty and merciless, and it does not spare anyone. In fact, good people suffer more than bad people. Today's unpredictable economy, downsizing, health, transfers, reorganizations, family issues, office politics, etc., can make even the most qualified employee unemployed. What if one door closes and another does not open? You are no different and are living in a fool's paradise without thinking about what will happen to you and your family if a disaster strikes you. Can you guarantee that you will not die or meet with any accident tomorrow?"

"You are scaring me, professor."

"Yes, didn't I tell you that this is a workshop to frighten executives? This is enough for today. Now go home, and let's meet again after one week."

I left his office in a daze. This surely was a frightening workshop, and the professor was right. How will my family manage if some disaster hits us? I was living in a fool's paradise and now definitely needed the professor's advice on what to do.

The Scary Questions

The next week was miserable. I started worrying about the professor's scary and valid questions. Soon, I was back in his office after a week. Now the professor handed me a paper with a bunch of questions to read and think about deeply.

- "Do you feel your lifestyle is going out of control?"
- "Do you feel overwhelmed by the number of things you have around your house?"
- "Are you exhausting yourself maintaining and babysitting them?"
- "Are you continuously spending money to catch up with your rich neighbors, co-workers, friends, and relatives?"
- "Do they have a strong influence on all of your purchases?"
- "Are you grappling with your finances and debt, or just wondering where your money disappears every month?"

- "Do you want to have better control over your income and expenditure?"

- "Are you above forty years of age? Are you facing periodic health problems and increasing medical expenses?"

- "Are you a salaried employee working in a high-pressure environment?"

- "Are there constant fears of downsizing, outsourcing, etc., in your organization or industry?"

- "Do you have any dependents to maintain? Are you worried about your or their future?"

"What is your answer to my questions?"

The professor's long list of disturbing questions and the previous week's scare got me thinking.

"Yes, professor, most of these apply to me. I have also been thinking about what we discussed last week. Such questions have started haunting me and are now giving me sleepless nights."

"Excellent, now you are on the right road. Why don't you now make some gradual to drastic changes in your lifestyle before it is too late?"

"But how do I make those gradual or drastic

lifestyle changes in this ruthless dog-eat-dog world? It's impossible!"

"Well, many things often seem unachievable until you give it a try."

"What do I need to do?"

"You should become a minimalist."

"How will that help?"

"It's the magic pill to eliminate or reduce most of your worries. Once you become a minimalist, you will be able to control your life regardless of what others around you think or do. Then you will be able to successfully,"

- Control unnecessary costs and simplify your life.

- Survive lengthy periods of unemployment and tackle retirement fears.

- Resist urges to spend unnecessarily and escape from the pressures of consumerism and obsession with useless material things.

- Lower your stress, obligations, and debt, and improve your health.

- Experience less cleaning, maintaining, and repairing the house.

- Control jealousy, envy, hate, and inferiority complex regardless of the millionaires and billionaires around you.

"Sounds interesting, professor. But I don't want to become stingy like my father or a saint and go to a forest. As Robert Frost said, I have promises to keep and miles to go before I sleep."

"Well, this is where you are mistaken. Most people think minimalism is just another fad like becoming a saint and running away to a forest. And some people think it is plain stinginess and live like a destitute. But you are mistaken. You don't have to embrace sainthood or stinginess to become a minimalist. You can have all the essential things in life and yet be a minimalist. Minimalism is mainly about controlling the number of material things you have or need in your life. It is a highly useful life discipline. And my lectures will show you how to achieve this discipline. But first, have a quick look at what is not minimalism to clear any hidden doubts you may still have."

- Minimalism is not leading a life of poverty when you are able to afford things.

- It is not about quitting your job, becoming a saint, and running away to a forest.

- It is not about living in an empty house or a tent without electricity, a phone, TV, computer, etc.
- It is not preventing your family and kids from having essentials like good schooling, books, or proper clothes.
- It is not about eating low-quality cheap food, removing your kids from school, stopping taking baths, etc.

"Finally, minimalism should not be viewed as a punishment you need to endure because you were born poor or committed sins in your previous life. Instead, it should be viewed as a life's financial discipline that will sail you through good and bad times. It can prevent you from being held hostage to loud-mouthed marketers, jazzy advertisements, paying extra for unnecessary frills, etc. It is aimed at achieving a method of thinking and a lifestyle that you can afford to live with for the rest of your life."

"Afford to live with for the rest of my life? That sounds valuable."

"Yes, it can also help you learn the difference between need and greed. And as you implement minimalism, it will also make you lighter and stronger. You will also gradually let go of your inevitable envy and jealousy created by constantly comparing yourself with those materially richer than you. To summarize, it will give you the mental strength and confidence to take a cold shower in the winter if necessary."

"Okay, sounds good. Let me give it a try. Now how do I become a minimalist, and how long does it take?"

"Becoming a minimalist is a gradual process that involves various changes in your lifestyle over a few months and years. It should be done slowly and steadily and cannot be done abruptly. In practical terms, minimalism is mainly about learning how to control two important things in your life, like,

- The wisdom to control obsession with material things in your life.
- The wisdom to control money in your life.

I will explain how you can achieve the two pearls of wisdom through a series of small lectures. You can interrupt to ask questions if necessary."

Lecture-1: The Big House Syndrome

"Most people desperately aspire to live in a big house. They think living in a palatial house will give them more happiness, and you can't blame them fully. This is because our materialistic society is conditioned to think that big is better and those who live in small houses must definitely be suffering because of their past sins. So, people constantly crave to move into a large house or feel jealous of those who live in palatial houses. And many people even take the risks of heavy loans to buy or build bigger houses. But does living in a big house really bring true happiness? The answer is a big NO."

"Why do you say no, professor?"

"To understand why, take the example of Mr. S who used to live with his wife and two high school kids in a compact and comfortable house in an ordinary area. He also had a lot of friends and neighbors in the area. However, as he moved up the corporate ladder, he became obsessed with material things and gradually increased his standard of living.

He sold his compact house and built a much bigger

house that was nearly five times the size of his old house in a posh area. Next, he built a swimming pool and an elevator, installed computers, TV sets, and air conditioners for every room, and got every possible electric and electronic gadget in his house. He also bought two big cars to keep up with his new status. With their new wealth, he and his family also gradually distanced themselves from their ordinary friends near his previous house. He thought his big house, fancy gadgets, and rich neighbors would make him and his family happy. But within a few months of the euphoria of living in a palace, he was invaded by many headaches."

"What headaches?"

"Now, instead of spending the weekends leisurely, he has to constantly deal with electricians, plumbers, carpenters, mechanics, pool cleaners, car drivers, repairmen, maids, security guards, servicemen, etc. Compared to the previous life, he now has more hassles, more stuff to maintain, more costs, and all his free time is spent babysitting the umpteen gadgets and other luxuries he now owns.

Within a couple of years, both his kids also moved away to faraway places for higher studies. By now, their old friends were also gone, and his rich neighbors didn't care. Now Mr. S and his wife were suddenly all alone in a lonely big house surrounded by tall compounds and unpredictable servants. In summary, Mr. S unknowingly moved from a simple life to a complicated life by increasing his material possessions. In addition, he was also now hit with a different kind of headache – the possibility of danger from criminals."

"What danger from criminals? Did he get robbed?"

"Fortunately, no. But have you ever taken a close look at the people who live in big palatial houses? If not, just visit any posh area in your city and observe the rich people for some days just for an academic exercise in minimalism. You will immediately notice that those rich people are hardly seen outside in their gardens, nor will you see their children playing outside, and nor will you see the owners chatting with their neighbors as you see in ordinary areas. In fact, you will not even see a shadow moving inside the big houses. All you will probably see is a lonely security guard guarding the house and a few expensive cars parked in front.

So, who and what are those rich people hiding from? Simple, they are now hiding from countless jealous eyes, criminals, freeloaders, and vagabonds who are now targeting their houses and kids. A lavish lifestyle always invites crime and other kinds of irritating troubles. This is why rich people who flaunt their wealth build tall compounds, install security cameras and guards, avoid people, constantly live in fear of untrustworthy servants, and get themselves into a golden prison. They will no longer be able to move around freely or deal with commoners like they could before they moved into a civilian palace. Now ask yourself if moving to a big house and inviting all those hassles is really worth it. Do you still think living in a big house is a joy?"

"But, hold on, professor! Does this mean I should never build a big house or upgrade my lifestyle even when I can afford it?"

"No, you don't have to be stingy and lead a life cramped in a tiny house when you can afford it. You can still build a good house and upgrade your lifestyle as long as your spending is based only on true needs and not on greed, status, and showing off to others. Secondly, you must consider the long-term maintenance capabilities of a big house. Ask if you can afford to successfully maintain a large house for years and decades. Where is the money going to come from? And if you are still having doubts or cynicism about my idealistic preaching of making you live in a small house, take the example of the billionaire, Warren Buffett."

"What does he do?"

"Warren Buffett, the CEO of Berkshire Hathaway, is one of the world's richest men with a net worth of more than 50 billion dollars. Yet, Warren Buffett hasn't let his $50 billion fortune go to his head. He still lives in an ordinary house that he bought in 1958, today valued at about a few hundred thousand dollars, while his billionaire friends live in gigantic multimillion-dollar houses with tall compounds, lawns, and dozens of security guards. He also drives an ordinary car purchased many years ago.

Does this mean Warren Buffett is a stingy miser? While it may appear so, the reality is he is neither stingy nor miserly. In fact, he donates billions of dollars to charity every year. The truth is he has mastered the art of creating wealth and rejecting unnecessary expenses. He knows the difference between necessity and luxury, and the difference between need and greed. This frugality has helped him grow his wealth exponentially."

"But surely he can live in a much bigger house as he is a billionaire, right?"

"Yes, he can. But when people ask him why he still stays in a small house when he can afford a palace, his answer is something like, 'Look, I don't want to manage 10 houses, and I don't want somebody else doing it for me, and I don't know why the hell I'd be happier. And an extra ten bedrooms are not going to make any difference.' This is the golden wisdom of a true minimalist. Now if Warren Buffett can do it despite having billions, surely you can also do it on a smaller scale. But you may argue that he can afford or pretend to be frugal because he already has enough wealth and need not worry about anything else. True, but do you know he has stayed the same way even when he was not a billionaire?

Therefore, as an aspiring minimalist, you should also try to imitate his simple methods on whatever financial scale you are in. For example, if you or your spouse is craving a new palatial house, first investigate whether the house you are living in is really insufficient for all your family members. Can it be expanded to make more space through some architectural changes and minor repairs? Is there too much useless stuff in your house occupying space and giving an impression that you are cramped for space? Can you afford to build or buy a new house? Will you still be able to maintain a big house in a few years or when you grow older? And so on. Only after evaluating your true needs and capabilities should you decide to make the jump."

"Good suggestions, professor. I never looked at the house from the long-run perspective. Now I understand. Maybe this was why my father refused to build or move to a bigger house even though we grumbled."

"Yes, your wise father could see long-term about his financial capacity to build and maintain a bigger house."

"You are right. Now I need to rethink moving to that new house. What's the guarantee that I will have sufficient income to maintain my lifestyle and repay the home loan for the next 20 years? Right now, I don't have any loan on my current house, and we have everything we need."

"Yes, think carefully and then make a move. Moving to a big house is a one-way street."

"What do you mean one-way street?"

"Do you remember the wife of the businessman?"

"Yes."

"Remember she refused to move to a smaller house and cooperate even though her husband was in deep financial trouble. The same situation may hit you also. Once your family gets accustomed to a big luxurious house, they will ferociously rebel against moving to a smaller house if you get into financial problems. You will have immense difficulties making them move down, as they will take you for granted and expect you to maintain an exponential lifestyle regardless of your financial difficulties."

"Hmm, but I am confident my family will support me if I get into difficulties."

"Really? Don't be so confident. Go home and do a small test stating you are having some financial troubles."

"What test?"

"Tell your kids to give up their iPads and smartphones and start using ordinary button phones. Also, tell them that you are canceling your Netflix subscription. Then tell your wife to stop using her car and use public transportation from now on."

"Wow! I need not do this test. I know the answer. They will not agree to this."

"Then how are you confident that they will support and cooperate with you when you get into real trouble?"

"Hmm, valid question. I will have a tough time

convincing them. Nobody will reduce their standards. Thanks for the scary lecture, professor. You opened my mind. I will put my new house dream on hold until I set my long-term finances right."

"Sorry for pouring cold water on your new house dreams. But unless you learn to think long term and have your finances right, you should not take such unnecessary mega financial risks just to impress others. This is enough for today. We shall meet after a few days."

Lecture-2: Downsizing and Retirement

"Today we shall discuss two inevitable things that will happen for any modern executive."

"What are they?"

"Downsizing and retirement."

"First question – Are you prepared for downsizing?"

"Hmm, that's a difficult question, professor. But there are constant fears of downsizing and reorganization in my industry."

"I know. This is why you need to be always prepared for downsizing even if the axe is not on your head now. In this unpredictable economy, even the best-qualified and most competent employees can lose their jobs. Do not assume that your excellent qualifications, experience, and wisdom will always get you a well-paying job. Even billionaires and Fortune 500 companies can get wiped out. So, unless you save money for a rainy day, you will be in deep trouble."

"How do I do that?"

"Simple, always spend less than you earn. Invest the difference in secure investments. This is the only way you can accumulate money for your future or a rainy day. The effects of losing a job can be shocking, especially if you have no second source of income. Oscar Wilde once said, 'It is better to have a permanent income than just be fascinating.' This is a very powerful message for everyone. When your income suddenly drops, life can become very chaotic not only for you but for all of your dependents. And it's not possible to depend on friends, relatives, and neighbors to run your livelihood for months and years when you are down. Just try borrowing money from someone when you are in trouble, and your faith in people will never be the same again. For example, if you were to lose your job tomorrow, how prepared are you?"

"How do I prepare for that?"

"Experienced financial consultants say you should always have enough money saved to cover at least six to nine months' worth of expenses in case you lose a job or cannot work for any reason. But my suggestion is you should think like a pessimist and aim for 12 to 18 months of expenses."

"How do I do that?"

"For example, suppose you are earning $5000 per month, and your monthly expenditure for the absolute essentials is $3000. Then you should make it a habit to save the remaining $2000 every month. This way, if you save for a year, you will have $24,000 with you. Suppose you lose your job, then this $24,000 will help you cover your monthly expenses for eight months while you look out for another job without going crazy. And if your job is less secure or layoffs are common in your industry, then you should save even more."

"Thanks, that's a good suggestion. I will do the calculations and start saving immediately."

"Now my second question. Are you prepared for retirement?"

"No, but that is still 15–20 years away."

"That is the mistake. Most people think retirement is far away and they need not worry about it till they cross fifty years of age. So, they lead a lavish life of purchases, vacations, eating out, etc., when they are young and earning well. But this is a dangerous mistake because time travels fast and retirement can hit you hard. A very large percentage of people have severe difficulties adjusting to retirement and a sudden drop in income."

"What sudden drop in income?"

"When you retire, your monthly income will abruptly stop and you will have to start living from your savings or on a small pension, right?"

"Correct."

"For example, have you ever imagined what it is to be old, retired, or have your monthly income drop to one-fifth or less than what you are earning today? Will you still be able to maintain the lifestyle you were accustomed to for many years? Do you have the courage to instantly downgrade your life? But with minimalism, you can get ready and be prepared for retirement many years before. So, think ten years, twenty years ahead, and imagine whether you will still be able to maintain the lifestyle you are currently leading."

"It's a scary thought."

"If you get a chill down your spine, then you need to quickly change your spending lifestyle to accommodate the future. Basically, when you reduce your lust for material things, you can be several steps ahead in tackling retirement."

"What's lust for material things?"

"We shall discuss that tomorrow."

Lecture-3: Cut the Clutter

"Today we shall discuss the craving for material things."

"Okay."

"Most people think having a lot of stuff and gadgets in their house will help save time or give them more enjoyment. This thinking is embedded in us because we are constantly bombarded by marketers 24 x 7. For example, if you see any TV or newspaper advertisement, it will keep showing a picture that you can become happier than before only if you own the latest smartphone, car, motorbike, or electrical gadget, and so on. And most people fall into such a marketing trap and increase the number of fancy things in their house.

But this is another big mistake because, beyond a certain essential limit, having more stuff around the house will actually make you miserable, poorer, and unnecessarily busy. Now ask yourself if you are also in the same boat on a small or equivalent scale. If yes, then you should take steps to minimize the number of things you own."

"How?"

"First, take an inventory of the things you own. Look around your house. Ask yourself questions like, do you think you have too many things lying around, are they occupying too much space, are they adding any value, are they making your life easier or more difficult, are they continuously costing money to maintain, etc.? If your answer is yes, then you should make a list of things that you can throw, donate, or sell away.

Less clutter around the house, the better it is for your health, peace of mind, and wallet. When you reduce stuff around the house, you will quickly experience happiness and lightness. It's like being stuck in traffic for hours and then experiencing the joy of seeing a free highway again. Start small, throw one or two things away every day, and gradually increase the numbers. Sometimes, you may even have to throw away things stealthily because your spouse or kids may not allow you to toss away any garbage even if they are defective or haven't been used in years."

"Yes, I think we have plenty of such stuff in our house."

"Also, decide when enough is enough. Cutting the clutter does not simply mean eliminating the unwanted material things around you. It also means eliminating certain responsibilities, obligations, and activities that hold you hostage daily. Today, the more you do, the more there is to do. The more responsibilities you take, the more tasks land on your head, and the expenditure increases. The more people you help, the more will line up to suck your blood. For example, imagine getting a phone call or an email every few minutes demanding your immediate attention, attending endless meetings, or always being in the midst of something critical or urgent, etc., at home or in the office. All these activities and involvement will not leave you any time to enjoy life even for a few hours without something or someone interrupting you.

Often, people take on extra responsibilities because they suffer from an inability to let go. Many people suffer from the indispensability syndrome to constantly prove or do something every day and every minute. They cannot bear being left out and always want to be involved in everything. They are terrified of being left out of the loop or some information. They are unable to delegate and believe nothing can work if they are not involved. Now ask if you are also in a similar category. If yes, you should take a pause and gradually cut down all such responsibilities and obligations by better delegation or completely eliminating them. When you reduce them, your costs will also come down. Remember, no one on their deathbed ever says, 'I wish I could have worked more.'"

"Good suggestions, professor."

"This is enough for today. Tomorrow we shall discuss the glorious day concept."

Lecture-4: Stop Dreaming of that Glorious Day

"What is that glorious day concept, professor?"

"People are conditioned to think that they first need abnormal amounts of money in their bank accounts to be happy. They dream of a day when all of their obligations will be fulfilled, all debts will be paid, all unfinished business will be completed, and immediately after that, they will get enough time to enjoy a leisurely life. Hence, people slog day and night for decades trying to make lots of money, get power, and status so they can have the freedom on some future glorious day to do what they love or dreamt to do for years."

"Yes, a lot of people do aim for that day."

"Sadly, by the time they get to that day, many years will have passed and they will only have the money and no friends, family, health, or time to enjoy it. However, in reality, most of you already have (or can have) many things that you want right now, except for maybe massive luxuries. But you just fail to see it."

"How?"

"Let me explain the story of a fisherman and the businessman. One day a fisherman was sitting lazily near a river trying to catch fish. A hard-working entrepreneur who was walking by noticed this and asked why this fellow was wasting time fishing instead of working hard and earning more money.

'You can't catch many fish the way you are doing,' said the entrepreneur.

The fisherman looked up and replied, 'What should I do for that?'

'Well, you should get bigger nets to catch more fish!' the entrepreneur answered.

'Then what will be my reward?' asked the fisherman.

The entrepreneur replied, 'You will make more money and also be able to buy a big boat that will help you to catch more quantities of fish!'

'Then what will be my reward?' asked the fisherman again.

The businessman got annoyed with the fisherman's silly questions but continued. 'You can buy a much bigger boat and also hire people to work for you!'

'Then what will be my reward?' repeated the fisherman.

The businessman now got angry. 'Don't you understand what I am saying? You can have a fleet of fishing boats, sail all over the world, and let your employees catch fish for you!'

Once again the fisherman asked, 'Then what will be my reward?'

The businessman was now furious and shouted at the fisherman, 'Don't you understand? You can become so rich that you won't have to work for your living again! You can spend all the rest of your days sitting on this river looking at the sun and fishing happily. You won't have a care in the world!'

The fisherman looked up and smilingly said, 'What do you think I'm doing right now?'

The entrepreneur suddenly felt like being hit with a truckload of wisdom and slowly walked away."

"Good story, professor. So, what do I need to do?"

"Though you may not want to go exactly the fisherman's way, what this interesting story teaches you is it is still possible to enjoy life whenever possible with what you currently have without always dreaming of that glorious day in the future. For example, thinking spiritually, if all your basic food, clothing, shelter, health, insurance, transportation, and a few other essential needs are currently taken care of, then you don't really need anything else in life, isn't it? But if you still don't agree and keep dreaming of acquiring terrific wealth, then look at it this way – Even if you have a dozen cars, how many will you drive at a time? Even if you own ten houses, how many will you stay in at a time? Even if you have a supermarket at home, how much food will you eat per day? Even if you have a hundred pairs of shoes, countless watches, and a massive wardrobe, how many sets will you wear per day? Even if you have a massive TV with a thousand channels and ten thousand movie DVDs, how many will you watch at a time? And even if you have a stubborn plan to enjoy each one of them in your life, you will soon run out of time, patience, and energy."

"Hmm."

"This is because the unavoidable law of diminishing returns will set in and you will unconsciously detach from them. Secondly, you will have to continuously slog to earn the tons of money necessary to maintain and protect all the luxuries you now own. So, when will you find time to enjoy your luxuries? It will become a Catch-22 situation where you will require a lot of money to buy all the luxuries you need, and earning a lot of money will take a lot of time and energy, and if you spend all your time and energy on earning that money, then you will not have any time and energy to enjoy those luxuries. Basically, there are two tragedies in a human's life. One is the suffering of not getting what your heart desires, and the second is the suffering of getting it. Hence, it is always advisable to be moderate in everything."

"You make a lot of sense, professor. Yes, it's a Catch-22 situation."

"Speaking in a lighter sense, even a child will agree that climbing from a lower level to a higher level is always a strenuous and anxiety-filled job. For example, climbing a regular ladder, a career ladder, a mountain, a steep staircase, or an airplane taking off, etc., are all anxiety-filled moments. But climbing down from a higher level to a lower level is a relief and brings joy and happiness. This is why a pilot and the passengers feel relieved when a plane lands safely. And these activities involve descending from a higher level to a lower level.

Similarly, in life, if you voluntarily aspire to go down in your lifestyle rather than constantly go up, then you will gradually become happier. As Steve Jobs once said in his famous Stanford speech, 'the heaviness of being successful was replaced by the lightness of being a beginner again, less sure about everything. It freed me to enter one of the most creative periods of my life.' If you understand this timeless wisdom of the saints and our forefathers, then you have already crossed the halfway mark of becoming a minimalist. Remember that even mighty empires and powerful dictators with huge palaces and exotic islands have all eventually crumbled to dust."

"Professor, now I can imagine what was going on in my father's eyes and mind. I feel sorry for calling him a penny-pincher."

"Well, enlightenment takes time. This is enough for today. We shall discuss spendthrifts tomorrow."

Lecture-5: Stop Being a Spendthrift

"Let me start my lecture by first defining spendthrifts."

"Okay."

"A spendthrift is a person who spends money recklessly and is extravagant in his or her nature. They are people who cannot control the urge to spend. For example, they will buy the latest phone even though they may already have two good working phones, or buy another pair of fancy shoes or new clothes even though their shoe rack or wardrobe is filled and spilling over. Spendthrifts also fall for personal loans and payments through credit cards. The idea of buying today and paying tomorrow is something few people can resist."

"Hmm, you are describing me, professor. A lot of my friends are also like this."

"But the downside is they will pile up debts that will never clear, and slowly such people will get into a nasty debt trap. In short, spendthrifts are freaks who have no control over their spending and only care about instant self-gratification or showing off to their friends. For example, countless celebrities lead a lavish lifestyle when they are earning tons of money and soon end up on a poor farm within a few years or finally commit suicide, unable to handle the psychological shock of losing their wealth and status. Now ask yourself if you or your family members are spendthrifts."

"Yes," I admitted sheepishly.

"Then you need to quickly change your spending habits and start saving money for your future needs. Today you may be strong, confident, and earning enough money, but is there any guarantee that you will still be earning enough money for the next twenty or thirty years? Unless you are filthy rich, it is very important to save money continuously to tackle emergencies, health problems, loan repayments, children's education, home repairs, retirement, and even your funeral expenses.

Just because you are earning a bundle today does not mean you should spend everything on luxuries and fancy living. You will never know what will hit you tomorrow or if the economy will go crazy. You should always be frugal in your spending and always concentrate on what is enough to 'meet a specific purpose' rather than what is 'nice to have.' Remember, frugality is not poverty, it is wisdom. For example, if you need a car for city transportation, a low-priced basic car serves the same purpose as an expensive fancy car. A simple rugged car serves the same purpose and is also softer on loan repayments, repair costs, and insurance when the axe falls on your monthly income."

"Sensible suggestion."

"Now let us discuss how you should purchase items. When buying any items, first evaluate the low, medium, and high types. For example, you can get an ordinary mobile phone for $100, a slightly better phone for $200, and a super-duper phone for $800. Minimalism is about choosing and living with the ordinary or slightly better phone. This way you will experience the joys of having a mobile phone but avoid the atrocious cost of a super-duper phone. You can also explore buying used goods. For example, if you are buying a book online, you can buy a new one for $14 or a used copy for less than $10. Both serve the same purpose."

"That's a good suggestion. Now I know why father used to first search for used items before we bought anything."

"My next suggestion is to earn more money. This

may not sound like a minimalist lifestyle suggestion. But this suggestion is not to encourage you to pursue greediness. Actually, more and more money is required even for just maintaining your existing minimalist lifestyle."

"How?"

"This is because of inflation and rising costs of everything. For example, an essential medicine that you could buy for 10 dollars last year may now cost 14 dollars. Hence, you need to increase your income to tackle such inflation. So,

- Invest in real estate and stocks in good companies.
- Invest in long-term fixed deposits, tax-free schemes, money-back policies, insurance schemes, and monthly income schemes.
- Have hobbies that can earn some money.
- Have a second income if possible and save income from that for a rainy day.
- Buy books on cost saving to learn about many new ways to earn, save, or reduce costs and taxes.
- Teach your family and kids the importance of frugality, saving, and earning money.
- Forcefully stop that burning desire to give

your family those unnecessary luxuries that your parents were unable or unwilling to provide. Remember, it is not mandatory to fulfill all their luxury desires.
- If you are the family breadwinner, ask them how they will manage things if you were to suddenly disappear tomorrow.
- Also, inspect your current lifestyle and the costs for each. Look around at what you drive, wear, eat, smoke, drink, and read. Are all of these really necessary? See whether you can cut or eliminate some of them.
- Drastically reduce credit card purchases and impulsive spending. With easy access to credit cards, people often buy useless goods, fancy items, expensive clothing, gadgets, and even cars because they don't feel the pinch of paying the full amount in cash.
- Explore solar power, rainwater harvesting, growing vegetables, etc.
- Ruthlessly cut on unnecessary things like entertainment, frequent eating out, and mandatory expensive vacations.
- When buying things you don't really need, it is better to think that you 'won't afford it'

rather than you 'can afford it.'
- Eliminate all unnecessary expenses like subscriptions to unwanted magazines, electronic gadgets, monthly payments, and so on.
- Don't invest all your money in high-risk investments even if they promise high returns. Invest only limited amounts you can afford to lose. It will be a disaster if you lose everything at a speculative risk. It's better to have a safe and lower return on your investments than a probable higher return with sleepless nights worrying about your money.
- Avoid unnecessary debt. Buy things that appreciate in value. Don't buy things that depreciate over time. Another bad thing is paying interest on a depreciating asset such as an automobile or a stereo set. Stereos, fancy clothes, automobiles, and electronic gadgets depreciate over time. Not only are you losing money by paying interest, but the item you are paying for is also losing value at the same time. That means you are losing money every day.
- Lead a simple life even if you are earning well.

Don't build a grand lifestyle and uplift your social and materialistic status by having an assumption that you will always make more and more money. You will never know when your lifeboat will start leaking. Always live within your sources of income.

- Have a budget for everything. When you live within a budget you can live better and without fear. Budgeting helps you understand where your money is coming from or where your money should go. Even if you create a nice manageable budget, keep looking for ways to cut unnecessary expenses.
- Finally, cultivate a lifestyle that you can afford to live with for the rest of your life."

"Whew! That was a long list of excellent suggestions, professor."

"Yes, all those suggestions are highly essential for a minimalist. My next suggestion is to stop living for others. A lot of people don't like minimalism because it doesn't seem practical in the surroundings they live in. But what they actually mean is they don't want to look weird in front of their friends and relatives. For example, not buying a car when all your friends and relatives have one may make you look like a miser or your kids may face some ridicule. But ask, who are you living for? Is it mandatory to meet everyone's expectations to avoid ridicule? Will they come to your rescue when you are down? The answer is no. Hence, you should stop the 'The neighbors have it, so we should also have it' thinking. Don't care about what others think about you not owning luxuries even if you can afford them. Consider whether you are buying something for a real need or just to impress someone. Let others keep the economy churning with their reckless spending. You don't bother. What really matters is you are willing and happy to spend only on essentials, but not on frills. When it comes to spending, remember what Will Rogers said, 'Too many people spend money they haven't earned, to buy things they don't want, to impress people they don't like.'"

"Great quote, professor."

"Yes, tomorrow we shall discuss celebrities."

Lecture-6: The Celebrity Myth

"Today we shall discuss famous celebrities."

"Okay."

"Most people think celebrities like movie stars, sportsmen, and pop stars don't have to worry about things like minimalism or frugality. But this is far from true, and minimalism is required even for such stars. Only extremely few celebrities can maintain their luxurious lifestyles for years and decades. For example, look at the rise and fall of some famous celebrities whose names you may have now forgotten.

MJ was a famous pop star but was supposedly $400 million in debt when he died unexpectedly in 2009. He also had to foreclose his famous Neverland home. He could not even pay the salaries of his employees. Reckless spending made him take loans, many of which he never paid back. MJ's money problems got worse once he got involved in numerous expensive lawsuits.

NC was one of Hollywood's biggest stars, earning $40 million at his peak, but also one of its biggest spenders. He purchased many houses, automobiles, and rare artifacts. The tax department fined him more than $6 million for failing to pay his 2007 tax bill. Cage's risky financial situation made him sell many of his personal belongings, including a treasured comic book.

MT was a heavyweight champion and earned $300 million when he was at the peak of his career but ended with a $23 million debt. He declared bankruptcy, had to go to jail, and went through rehab before he again reached financial stability. By 2003, he owed tons of money to the IRS, British tax authorities, lawyers, personal trainers, financial managers, music producers, and several others.

AK was a famous actor. With 200+ films under his belt, he was a well-known face of Indian cinema. However, even his fame couldn't keep the hard times at bay. Late in his life, AK went bankrupt and couldn't even pay his basic medical bills."

"Wow, imagine earning millions and losing everything."

"Yes. Similarly, there are many celebrities in sports, films, etc., worldwide who have met the same fate. I have created a small table that summarizes the rise and fall of celebrities."

Age	Status
20 years	Annual income – Five million dollars, luxurious lifestyle, fancy cars, mansions, advertisements, sponsorships, name, and fame
22 years	Annual income – Four million dollars, Dip in popularity starts
24 years	Annual income – One million dollars, rapid reduction in fan base, fame, and new opportunities
26+ years	Out of the limelight, forgotten by the media and public, sporadic income, high debts, unable to maintain a lifestyle, depression, drugs, etc.

"This is an amazing table, professor."

"See, when even top celebrities who earn millions can collapse it's very easy for normal people like you and me to also fall down if we are not careful. That's enough for today. Let us discuss smartphones tomorrow."

Lecture-7: The Smartphone Story

"Do you know how smartphones can suck your wallet?"

"Yes, they are expensive but are indispensable in today's world, professor."

"I know, but have you done a calculation of how much it actually costs a family of four in a year and over the years?"

"No."

"Okay, let's do that. First look at the specifications of a new smartphone," said the professor and handed me a piece of paper.

Great Company Launches Great Smartphone at Great Price

- Huge Six Feet Bulletproof Screen.
- 100 ghz Processor.
- 1000 GB Internal storage expandable to 50,000 GB.
- 100,000 x 80,000 p insanely high resolution.
- 500MP Front and Back Camera to shoot your

own full-length 3D movie.
- 25 SIM slots.
- 50,000mAh battery with 10,000 hours of continuous talk time.
- Supports 2G, 3G, 4G to16G
- Only 12 kg weight.

"Do such advertisements sound familiar?"

"Hah, these are ridiculous specifications, professor."

"Yes, I know. I was just exaggerating but there is no way to hide from such advertisements today."

"Yes, we do get bombarded with plenty of such ads."

"Nowadays it is very common to see entire families owning smartphones enabled with internet connections. And according to my own unverifiable estimates, 80% of smartphone users spend 80% of their time addicted to the following online activities from the time they wake up to the time they go to sleep.

1. Check their personal emails every three minutes.
2. Upload a selfie, photo, video, or like something

Lecture-7: The Smartphone Story

on Facebook and other sites continuously and read the comments.

3. Instantly watch some funny video that went viral on YouTube.
4. Immediately forward a joke on WhatsApp to all your 650 contacts and read all their funny replies, LOLs, and OMGs.
5. See what important hashtag you missed on Twitter in the last five minutes and quickly tweet your stunning opinion.
6. Sit in heavy traffic fuming and calculate the length of the traffic jam in kilometers while listening to some free online music.
7. Check important information like the specs of the next shiny Smartphone that got released this morning.
8. Download a new cool ringtone or play some game or some useful app like checking the temperature on different planets.
9. Occasionally, look for some information like news summaries, some educational stuff, or some latest breaking news from Timbuktu, etc.

Though smartphones have many advantages have you ever calculated what it is really costing a modern family of four to do the above online activities daily? No idea? Then let us run through some numbers assuming zero inflation on costs of handsets and usage charges. These calculations are based on the prices of handsets and usage plans available in the market today. But first, you need to let me know which Smartphone family you belong.

If you are from the Apple family

Cost of the Smartphone: US$500 to US$1500 each.

Total cost of handsets for your family: US$2000 to US$6000.

Average monthly bill: US$60 to US$80 per month per phone.

Annual usage costs for your family: US$2880 to US$3840.

Handset life: Two years assuming your family is able to resist the temptation of that dazzling new smartphone on sale now. But if you can't resist then add the costs of four new handsets at the beginning of the third year. Add some extra costs for screen guards, flip cases, extra chargers, paid apps, etc.

Conclusion: If you go by the same calculations your family will end up spending whopping sums of money on your smartphone usage for years and years.

If you are from the Android family

Cost of the Smartphone: U$$300 to U$1000 each.

Total cost of handsets for your family: US$1200 to US$4000.

Average monthly bill: US$60 to US$80 per month per phone.

Annual usage costs for your family: US$2880 to US$3840.

Handset life: Two years assuming your family is able to resist the temptation of that dazzling new smartphone on sale now. But if you can't resist then add the costs of three new handsets at the beginning of the third year. Add some itsy bitsy costs for screen guards, flip cases, extra chargers, paid apps, etc.

Conclusion: If you go by the same calculations your family will end up spending whopping sums of money on your smartphone usage for years and years.

"Wow! I never realized that we are paying so much

for our smartphone usage, professor."

"Shocked? As you can see people will soon end up being smartphone rich and cash poor. So, this is how money drains out of your pocket continuously. Finally, we shall end this lecture with a famous quote from Edward Romney who says - *The urge to spend all you make is called consumer mentality. Try to get an investment mentality instead.* That's enough for today. Tomorrow, we shall learn some practical methods of minimalism.

Lecture-8: Practical Examples

"Today I will give a bunch of suggestions that you can explore in your journey to minimalism. Adopt whatever you can, either now or later.

1. *Big house* to a *small house*. For example, if you are staying in a big rented house see if you can shift to a small compact house.
2. Hundreds of stuff in your house to just enough stuff. See what stuff you can throw or sell that can make your house lighter and airier.
3. *Big expensive car* to a *small-medium car*. Less maintenance and insurance costs.
4. *Buying vegetables* to *grow them* in your yard. If you have space in your garden, you can enjoy the happiness of growing vegetables.
5. *Expensive gym*-to-*home exercises*. Why waste money in a gym when you can downsize your weight through simple home exercises?
6. Buying *new goods* to buying *used goods*. Why waste money on new goods when good second-hand stuff is available for half the price?

7. High-speed *expensive internet* connection to low-cost basic connection. Ask do you really need a blazing internet connection or can you live with a basic or medium connection?
8. Vacation *every year* to *occasional* vacation. Ask is it mandatory to go on exotic or expensive vacations every year. Can't you spend the holidays peacefully at home or travel to nearby low-cost destinations?
9. Dozens of clothes and shoes or just enough clothes and shoes.
10. Travel by *personal car* to *public transportation* or cycling or carpooling.
11. Aim for a substantial reduction in electricity, water, and fuel consumption. Switch off computers and gadgets when not in use.
12. Multiple newspapers and magazines to one newspaper and magazine.
13. Buy items that have a resale value. You can sell them after use and recover a percentage of the money.
14. Also, note that you need not always buy the cheapest item. Buying a durable item even if it is expensive will save money in the long run instead of buying a cheap item that will break soon.

15. Junk food to healthy foods. Stop eating junk foods that spoil your health and increase medical expenses. Try healthy foods.
16. Health improvement through natural and herbal medicines instead of expensive medicines from top companies. Most simple to medium ailments have low-cost herbal medicines that can be equal to or better than fancy medicines.
17. Cook at home instead of eating out. Avoid frequent parties. Controlling the urge to have lavish parties to impress your friends and relatives.
18. Learn simple household repairs to avoid spending a fortune on servicemen.
19. Avoid buying stuff in supermarkets if you want just one or two items. Go to small shops. This is because you will end up buying many unwanted items in the supermarket along with the items you need.
20. Similarly, you can improve on this list and explore several other ways to cut costs and headaches.

"Your suggestions are excellent, professor. I had never thought of all these ways of saving money."

"Tomorrow we shall see some magnificent gems

like before."

"Great! I look forward to them."

Some Magnificent Gems

Similar to my earlier workshop the professor started displaying all the famous quotes he had collected regarding frugality.

I'm a practitioner of elegant frugality. I don't feel comfortable telling other people what to do, so I just try and lead by example - Amory Lovins

Wealth consists not in having great possessions, but in having few wants - Epictetus

Frugality includes all the other virtues - Cicero

Annual income twenty pounds, annual expenditure nineteen six, result happiness. Annual income twenty pounds, annual expenditure twenty pound ought and six, result misery - Charles Dickens

You must gain control over your money or the lack of it will forever control you - Dave Ramsey

Don't tell me what you value, show me your budget, and I'll tell you what you value - Joe Biden

I'd like to live as a poor man with lots of money. -

Pablo Picasso

If we command our wealth, we shall be rich and free. If our wealth commands us, we are poor indeed - Edmund Burke

I have learned to seek my happiness by limiting my desires, rather than in attempting to satisfy them - John Stuart Mill

He who will not economize will have to agonize - Confucius

Being frugal doesn't mean slashing your spending or depriving yourself of things that you enjoy. It means knowing the value of a dollar and making every effort to spend it wisely - Frank Sonnenberg,

Beware of little expenses; a small leak will sink a great ship - Benjamin Franklin

Being frugal does not mean being cheap! It means being economical and avoiding waste -Catherine Pulsifer

There are plenty of ways to get ahead. The first is so basic I'm almost embarrassed to say it: spend less than you earn - Paul Clitheroe

Don't tell me where your priorities are. Show me

where you spend your money and I'll tell you what they are – James W. Frick

The most substantial people are the most frugal, make the least show, and live at the least expense - Francis Moore

You understand a whole lot about money when there isn't any. What you learn is that money is hard to come by, and it is important not to waste it - Jack Bogle

There is no dignity quite so impressive and no independence quite so important as living within your means - Calvin Coolidge

If you buy things you do not need, soon you will have to sell things you need - Warren Buffett

If saving money is wrong, I don't want to be right - William Shatner

Money? How did I lose it? I never did lose it. I just never knew where it went - Edith Piaf

Finally, the professor said.

"This concludes your frugality workshop, my young chap. I hope you found my coaching useful and will start using my suggestions diligently. Before you go, let me give you some advice. Finally, as with every life's discipline, there will be some hardships and downsides to minimalism as well.

1. You may have difficulties adjusting to minimalism for some time. So, start slowly without causing grief to anyone. Your family members must get accustomed to minimalism slowly and not abruptly or they will rebel and cause problems for you.
2. You may find it difficult to get consent from your family and kids as they may be accustomed to a richer lifestyle. You may face ridicule and rebellion from family, friends, neighbors, and relatives.
3. Remember, the businessman story where his wife refused to downgrade her life even though her husband was deep in debt and stress? Secondly, the husband was also at fault for giving his family wealth and luxury beyond what he could manage or afford for years and years.
4. You may regret some decisions because you may miss out on some enjoyment.

But look at the bright side. Nothing great in life is achieved without sacrifice. You have to sacrifice something in order to get something better from life. All you have to say is "**Challenge Accepted**" and go ahead. Remember the one who pays makes the rules. Learn to say a firm NO without any guilt or regret for all non-essentials. Do not assume that you have to somehow slog and fulfill all their demands and desires. So, don't promise that you will get it done when you get your next salary, bonus, etc. If you do that, then they will pester you till you get it done.

Always remember that the breadwinner's primary responsibility is mainly to provide ESSENTIAL food, clothing, and shelter. All luxuries and non-essentials are OPTIONAL. Over time you will realize that saving money and downshifting is also as joyful as earning and spending money. All the tips and suggestions that I explained are nothing new and have been practiced by our wise forefathers for decades. This is why they were able to survive and sustain themselves in spite of earning a meager salary compared to today's mega salaries. Now I shall explain what was going on in your father's mind."

"Yes, I would like to know that, professor."

"Your father believed that his primary responsibility was only to fulfill your basic food, clothing, and shelter. He had your long-term interests in mind. This is why he did not succumb to any demands for luxuries just to hear his family squeal in delight. He knew that his earnings, health, and physical strength would not be stable for years and decades. He did want you to come to the streets if some mishap happened to him. This is why I said he was wise and a long-distance runner in life and not a short-distance runner. His eyes and mind could see life threats, risks, and dangers that you (and your friends and relatives) were unable or unwilling to see."

"Thanks a lot, professor. This was the second-best workshop that I have attended in my life. I can now clearly see what was going on in my wise father's mind. It was because of his tough frugality that our family was able to survive for so many years without getting into any serious financial troubles. I now know how was able to manage the household expenses even when he was frequently unemployed and bedridden with sickness. Had he been a spendthrift we would have come to the streets decades ago. I will no longer insultingly call him a penny-pincher. But I do wish he had explained this to us."

"You would not have understood just like how

your kids will not understand if you try to explain to them. But it's your duty to ensure that they do not come to the streets by succumbing to your and their desires for luxuries. This is my old-fashioned advice, but you know that old is gold and also bold."

"Thanks a lot, professor. I will immediately start implementing your suggestions. You have opened my eyes."

Other Books by the Author

Personal Planner

Personal Disaster Preparedness Planner
Organize your Information, Belongings, and Activities to Protect your Family in a Crisis

Humor Books

Become a Dictator
A Short and Snappy Guide

Become a Modern Artist
The Greatest and Easiest Job on Earth

Big Money
Top Secret Guide to the Stock Market Circus

The Mirage Peddlers
How to Become an Advertising Guru

The Mud Horse
Fantastic Jobs for Firebrand Feminists

Spirituality Books

The Miracle Law
The Pristine Path to Purpose and Prosperity

The Inventor of Nothing
A Mild and Wild Chat with the Brilliant Cosmic Designer

Personal Development Books

The Power of Laziness
Discovering the Wisdom of Slowness

The Extreme Minimalist
Discovering the Joys of Minimalism and Frugality

Get to the Point
A Short and Snappy Guide

The Curses of a Thousand Mothers
How We Pursue Joyful Sins

The Long Fuse
Why the Buddha Never Took Aspirin

No Easy Future!
Seven Habits to Tackle Tomorrow

The Compass Mind
A Short Guide to Think in All Directions

Start Saying NO!
How to Stop Living for Others and Start Pursuing your Goals

The Gibraltar Briefcase
The Wise Weapons of Exceptional Executives

The Glass Prison
The How to Stay Productive during a Lockdown

Children Books

Secret Trip to a Jolly Jungle
The Adventures of Tommy and his Magic Spaceship

Secret Trip into the Ocean
The Adventures of Tommy and his Magic Spaceship

Secret Trip to a Treasure Island
The Adventures of Tommy and his Magic Spaceship

Secret Trip to Outer Space
The Adventures of Tommy and his Magic Spaceship

Other Books by the Author

The Magic Apple and his Mighty Friends

Technology Books

IT Asset Management
A Practical Guide for Technical and Business Executives

Disaster Recovery and Business Continuity
A Quick Guide for Organizations and Business Managers

Practical IT Service Management
A Concise Guide for Busy Executives

Fiction Books

FINK!
The Mafia's Nightmare

The Patriot's Confession
A Spy Thriller

The World's Shortest Novels
The Sixty Seconds Bookshelf

Personal Development Magazine
Wealth of the Wise

All the above books are available in both Paperback and eBook on all major book retailers

Author Services

Become an Author Course - Do you dream of becoming an Author? Do you want to share your Knowledge, Imagination, or Experience and write your first Fiction or Non-Fiction Book? Then take my Self-Paced Video Course on Thinkific for just US$79.95. The link is below.

https://thejendra.thinkific.com/courses/how-to-become-an-author-and-self-publish-your-book

Publish your Book Project - If you have already written a book and want to publish it, then I can help you to Self-Publish it Worldwide on Amazon, Apple, Kobo, BN, Google Play, Flipkart, and other book retailers in both Paperback and all eBook formats through my unique Assisted Self Publishing method.

Visit http://www.author-world.com for details

About the Author

Good day. My name is **Thejendra Sreenivas**. I was a Technology Manager in the IT industry for nearly 30 years. Before entering the IT industry, I was also an electronics lecturer for a short duration.

I have written and self-published 35+ books on various subjects. All my books are available in both Paperback and Kindle on Amazon and as an eBook on Apple, Kobo, B&N, Google Play, and many other retailers. I am also the Editor and Publisher of a font-optimized digital magazine called **Self Improvement International** which contains articles on personal development, workplace issues, humor, writing, and publishing.

I am now a **Book Publishing Coach** and offer services like *Assisted Self-Publishing, Manuscript Formatting, Facebook Ads, Ghostwriting, One Page Websites, Article Writing, and Podcast Creation.* In addition, I also offer Personal Development Coaching.

Please visit my web cave - **www.thejendra.com** or **www.author-world.com** for details of my books, magazine, and coaching information.

Online Courses by the Author

www.ingramcontent.com/pod-product-compliance
Lightning Source LLC
Chambersburg PA
CBHW021455210526
45463CB00002B/782